SHIPS
From Start to Finish

Ryan A. Smith

Photographs by Jim Pidgeon and NASSCO/Ken Wright

BLACKBIRCH PRESS

An imprint of Thomson Gale, a part of The Thomson Corporation

THOMSON
™
GALE

Detroit • New York • San Francisco • San Diego • New Haven, Conn. • Waterville, Maine • London • Munich

THOMSON
GALE

© 2005 Thomson Gale, a part of The Thomson Corporation.

Thomson and Star Logo are trademarks and Gale and Blackbirch Press are registered trademarks used herein under license.

For more information, contact
Blackbirch Press
27500 Drake Rd.
Farmington Hills, MI 48331-3535
Or you can visit our Internet site at www.gale.com

Photo Credits: Cover (main and inset), pages 6, 7, 8, 9 (main and inset), 10, 11 (main and inset), 13, 14, 15, 16, 17, 18, 19 (main and inset), 20, 21, 25 (inset), 26–27 © Jim Pidgeon; pages 3, 4, 22, 25 (main), 28, 29, 31 © NASSCO/Ken Wright; pages 5, 13 (inset) Courtesy of NASSCO; page 24 Courtesy of Wartsila Lips; page 30 AP Wide World Photos.

LIBRARY OF CONGRESS CATALOGING-IN-PUBLICATION DATA

Smith, Ryan A., 1974–
  Ships : from start to finish / by Ryan A. Smith.
    p. cm. — (Made in the USA)
  ISBN 1-4103-0456-6 (hardcover : alk. paper)
  1. National Steel and Shipbuilding Company, A General Dynamics Company (San Diego, Calif.) 2. Shipbuilding—United States. 3. Naval architecture—United States. I. Title. II. Series: Made in the U.S.A.

  VM301.N28S65 2005
  623.82'4—dc22   2004018839

Printed in United States
10 9 8 7 6 5 4 3 2 1

Contents

Dedication
To my mom, dad, and sister.

Special Thanks
The publisher and author would like to thank Gary Brashears, Jim Pidgeon, Kenneth Wright, Jim Scott, Linda Keener, and the entire staff of thousands at NASSCO for their generous help in building this book.

Ships are giant machines. They are used to transport heavy equipment, products, and people across the ocean. Ships can handle severe storms and huge ocean waves. Some ships can travel more than 15,000 miles (24,140km) on a single load of fuel. That means a ship can go from California to China and back without refueling.

It takes a large crew of sailors to keep a ship running properly. People sometimes live on ships for many months at a time, even years.

But how are ships made?

A navy ship cuts a wide wake as it cruises the Pacific Ocean.

NASSCO

The National Steel and Shipbuilding Company (NASSCO), a General Dynamics company, builds large oceangoing ships. NASSCO has made more than 100 ships since opening. NASSCO is never closed, and people work there in shifts around the clock.

The NASSCO shipyard in San Diego, California, is huge! Thousands of people work at NASSCO. NASSCO covers 80 acres of land and 46 acres of ocean water. NASSCO even has its own post office, fire department, hospital, gas station, training school, fix-it shop, and recycling center.

An aerial view of the NASSCO shipyard shows its immense size.

Uses for Ships

Many ships are used to transport cargo and products around the world. Most countries rely on ships to import and export products at ports. Tanker ships can carry over 1 million barrels of oil. Other ships transport cars, food, toys, clothes, appliances, and electronics. In fact, ships carry almost everything in your home.

Some ships are used for naval purposes. Some navy ships are very fast, while others are large and slow. The largest navy ships built at NASSCO can carry thousands of soldiers, along with 100 tanks and 900 trucks. Others might have missiles or rockets attached to them. Some ships even carry fleets of helicopters and airplanes overseas, and have special take-off and landing areas on the deck!

Navy ships like this carry military helicopters and airplanes overseas.

Planning to Build

Ships are carefully designed before they are built. At NASSCO, each ship is built according to strict plans. Engineers use complex math and computer programs to create a blueprint (a detailed plan) of each ship. Sometimes a small wooden model of the ship is made during the planning stage.

Engineers and supervisors hold a planning meeting (opposite page) before a ship is built at NASSCO. Wooden pieces (above) are sometimes used to build a small model of a planned ship.

SHIP FACT

Some ships can carry more than 2.5 million gallons (9.46 million liters) of fuel. That's about the same as 10,000 Olympic-sized swimming pools!

Steel

It usually takes one to two years to build just one ship. Most of the ship is made of steel. Thousands of tons of steel are necessary to build a single ship. Trains and diesel trucks deliver large sheets of steel from mills in California, Pennsylvania, and Oregon. Then a giant magnetic crane grabs the steel sheets and drops them into the raw-steel yard.

When it is time to build a ship, the magnetic crane will pick up the steel and carry it onto a set of tracks. The tracks move the sheet through the Wheelabrator. The Wheelabrator is like an automated car wash for the steel sheets. It cleans the rust and dirt from the raw steel. Then every sheet is painted and code numbers are added. The code numbers tell the shipbuilders which part of the ship each sheet will become when it leaves the Wheelabrator.

Opposite: *A magnetic crane prepares to drop steel sheets into the raw-steel yard.*
Above: *The Wheelabrator (inset and main) cleans, paints, and adds code numbers to the large steel sheets.*

Small Parts

Small parts are created from some of the steel sheets. Engineers use computers to design and improve the small parts. Machines are programmed to automatically cut out pieces of steel like cookie cutters. The underwater burner is one machine that cuts steel into small pieces. It burns through the thick steel underwater to reduce the amount of smoke released into the air. The small pieces of steel are cleaned and painted with new code numbers that tell where each piece will be used.

Opposite: A worker creates small parts with the gas burner.

Above: The underwater burner cuts through steel underwater to reduce smoke.

Right: Painted code numbers tell where every part will be used.

History of NASSCO

In 1905, George C. Ort and Leon Boethell opened a small machine shop in San Diego called California Iron Works. The shop primarily manufactured structured steel for framing multistory buildings, but also made manhole covers, fire hydrants, ocean buoys, and many other molded steel products. After moving to an oceanfront location in 1945, the small steel company took on the monstrous task of building boats, barges, and oil rigs, and became the National Steel and Shipbuilding Company (NASSCO).

In 1960, NASSCO decided to focus on building only large, oceangoing ships. NASSCO made more than 100 ships between 1960 and 2005 for the U.S. Navy and commercial customers, and is the largest shipbuilder on the West Coast of the United States.

SHIP FACT

The first boat built at the bayside NASSCO property was a 52-foot (15.85m) fishing boat named Juana. The 40-ton boat was completed in 1945, and used for tuna fishing.

Opposite: NASSCO has been building ships for sixty years in San Diego. The fishing boat Juana (inset) was the first boat built at NASSCO.

Forming Steel

While small parts are cut from some cleaned and coded steel sheets, other sheets go from the Wheelabrator to a gas burner. The gas burner slices the sheets into long steel strips. Then the steel strips are curved with the ship's frame bender machine. These long, curved strips will be the ship's channels. The channels will make up the frame of the hull, giving it form and strength like a skeleton.

Left: *The ship's frame bender machine curves a channel, an important part of a ship's hull.*

Right: *Curved strips of steel like these make a ship sturdy.*

The Hull

Some steel sheets will become the hull of the ship. Engineers carefully plan every hull design. The hull is the bottom shell of the ship, and makes the ship float.

Large steel sheets are curved according to the ship's blueprint. The sheets are placed side by side on the ground and welded together to form big pieces of the hull. Then channels are welded to the new walls of steel to reinforce them. The large steel pieces of the hull are lifted into place by a crane. Then they are all welded together to form the ship's walls and seal water out. The hull is then painted any colors its new owner wants.

Curved sheets of steel fit together like puzzle pieces to form a ship's hull.

Welding

Every piece of steel on a ship is held together by a process called welding. Steel parts are bonded by melting them together with a welding machine. Between the steel pieces, welders melt thin strips of steel that act like very strong glue when they cool. Welded steel is airtight and watertight.

Over 1,000 welders work at NASSCO. Welders work on every part of the ship. Welders must always wear protective clothing, including gloves, a helmet, and a face shield, while working.

A welder wears gloves and a face shield to protect himself.

Building the Blocks

Some steel shapes will form big blocks. Every block is a small piece of the ship. Blocks form the ship's oil tanks, engine room, living quarters, galley (kitchen and rest area), the bridge (control room), and more. Each block is made of steel, small parts, pipes, pumps, and machines. A single block can weigh over 500 tons!

Opposite: A worker welds parts of a block together.

Above: A finished block can weigh more than 500 tons.

Right: The pump being added to this block will push fluids throughout the ship.

The Pipe Shop

Pipes for the ship are fitted (hooked together) at the pipe shop. The pipes will carry water, oil, natural gas, sewage, exhaust, and fuel through the ship. All sizes of metal pipe are bent and welded together at the pipe shop.

The finished pipe pieces are cleaned in an acid bath. Then the pipes are tested for leaks. Some ships use more than 250,000 feet (76,200m) of pipes. That's almost 50 miles (80.5km) of pipes!

Left: *A welder fits pipes together inside the pipe shop.*

Opposite: *A worker lowers pipes into an acid bath to clean them.*

Engines

Engines are usually installed in the ship during the middle of the ship-building process. Most times, an engine is placed into the bottommost section of the stern (back), inside the completed hull. Cranes lift each engine piece into the hull and place it in the engine room. The engine pieces are put together by mechanics before the engine is checked and tested.

Several different types of engines are used on ships, including gas turbines and diesels. The engine type depends on a ship's size and mission. The engine must be powerful enough to operate the ship properly yet not be too bulky or heavy.

Most modern ships use diesel engines. Diesels offer good fuel economy and can be built to any specific size. The biggest diesels installed by NASSCO produce more than 20,000 horsepower. That is about 70 times more powerful than the average American car engine!

Opposite: Most ships use powerful diesel engines like these.

Propellers

Propellers are usually installed once all the engines are placed. Bronze propellers are used to power the ships through the ocean. An average ship propeller is 22 feet (6.7m) wide and weighs more than 26 tons! Most of the propellers are cast (molded from molten bronze) in Holland by a company called Wartsila Lips. The propellers are shipped overseas to NASSCO on a ship. A single propeller costs $250,000!

Left: Huge bronze propellers shipped to NASSCO from overseas power the ships.

Opposite: Propellers are connected to the bottom rear of a ship (inset and main) once the engines are in place.

SHIP FACT

Ships are expensive. A tanker ship costs about $100 million, and some U.S. Navy ships cost more than $200 million each!

Moving Blocks

Giant cranes are used to place each finished block inside the hull. Two cranes lift a block high above the ship. Then the cranes carefully lower the block into the hull. Each crane can carry up to 300 tons, or more than 1.3 million pounds (272,155kg)!

Blocks are lined up side by side inside the ship and then welded to each other. A second level of blocks is stacked on top of the first, and those are welded together. Then a third level is added and welded. Levels of blocks are stacked until the hull is completely filled to the top.

Left: *Two 300-ton cranes lower a block into the ship's hull.*

Adding the Deck

The ship's deck (main floor) is constructed when all the blocks are inside the hull. The upper level of blocks contain pieces of the deck. Other pieces of the deck are carried into place by cranes. The deck pieces fit together like a giant jigsaw puzzle when all of the blocks are in place. Then the pieces are welded to seal all levels of the ship.

Cranes carry a piece of the ship's deck into place.

The Bridge

The bridge (control room) is the most important compartment of any ship. The bridge is the command center for most operations on board. It is like the cockpit of an airplane. In the bridge, the captain, navigators, and driver send commands to the engine room to direct the ship.

The bridge is added after the deck is completed. Each bridge is built at NASSCO as a block. Then it is lifted onto the stern of the ship with cranes. The bridge is welded to the deck before all the electronics, wires, pipes, and computers are connected.

The bridge is added to the ship once the deck is completed. It is the most important room on the ship.

Bon Voyage

Every part, pipe, pump, and machine is thoroughly checked and tested for problems before a ship is considered complete. After all the tests are successful, the ship can be released to its new owner.

A huge party takes place when a ship is completed and ready to leave the shipyard. Many people come to NASSCO to celebrate the birth of each giant ship. It is traditional to smash a bottle of champagne across the bow (front) of every new ship. The new ship can sail away after the party is over.

Completed ships are pulled away from the docks at NASSCO by tugboats. Then the tugboats guide each new ship out of San Diego Harbor and into the Pacific Ocean.

Above: *People break bottles of champagne on the bow of a new ship to celebrate its birth.*

Opposite: *Tugboats guide a finished ship away from the NASSCO shipyard.*